CONTENTS

INTRODUCTION

Have you ever heard of Jack the Ripper? Probably. In the days of Queen Victoria he killed around eight people and then vanished. He was never caught. Dozens of books have been written about him, there have been movies and television programmes and plays. There have even been jokes written about him. Try this one on your teacher ...

Jack was an evil killer who you would NOT want to meet in the misty and greasy, gas-lit cobbles of old Victoria's London. He was a villain. He wasn't a hero or someone you'd like to take home to tea.

But the world *remembers* him.

And have you heard of Edmund Reid? No? He was a hero. In 1877 he was the first man to jump from a hot-air balloon with a parachute. Parachutes would go on to save thousands of lives. But would you want to be the FIRST brave person to try one out?

Edmund Reid made 23 balloon flights and broke a world record. Such a man of courage. Edmund Reid was also a policeman – the policeman who *failed* to catch Jack the Ripper.

You see? Most people remember the villain, Jack. Most people have never even heard of Edmund, the hero. How unfair is that?

But that's history. The evil men and women are usually remembered – the great and the good are often forgotten.

The world just seems to love villains. Who were the 50 worst in the distant days of the past? Read on and find out ...

Vicious Villain
Tip 1

Top assassin tip

Want to kill a king? You can't get near them. There are always bodyguards around them. Bodyguards go everywhere ... except the toilet! So kill the king in the royal loo. In 1016 King Edmund Ironside made the mistake of going to the toilet...

1 While the king feasts, go to the toilet pit.

2 Lie down with your knife in your hand (never mind that you are lying in other people's poo).

3 When the king sits over the toilet pit strike upwards with your knife, through his bum into his bowels.

4 Escape. Have a bath. Have another bath.

One report says the killer paid two servants to stick an iron hook into the king's bowels.

 8

YOUNG VILLAINS

Many villains were just nasty from the moment they were born. If you want to be a top terror, it helps to be born a villain and to grow up doing villainous things from an early age.

EMPEROR ELAGABALUS

Roman emperor (AD 203–222)

His **savage** story

🦠 This terrible tot's mummy made him the high priest of Elagabalus, the sun god. That meant he sacrificed hundreds of sheep and cattle in the temple and then poured rich wine over the blood-dripping bodies.

🦠 So he grew up a bit 'odd'. After a while the sad lad really began to believe he WAS the sun god and changed his name to Elagabalus. You wouldn't believe the things he did. Or would you?

His **wicked** ways

Can you match up these bits of Elagabalus's nasty life?

1. He sacrificed ...

2. He studied ...

3. He put wild cats into ...

4. He played games where prizes were ...

5. He rewarded dancers with ...

6. He punished a slave with ...

7. He smothered guests with ...

8. He terrified a crowd with ...

9. He made his friends wrestle with lions and eat ...

10. He tied his enemies to a wall so he could stab them with ...

A. rose petals

B. scorpions

C. dead dogs

D. the guts of dead children

E. the bedrooms of friends

F. live parrots

G. poisonous snakes

H. children

I. red-hot pokers

J. starving rats

Answers:

1H) He started to sacrifice children in the temples but he only killed children who still had TWO parents so there was twice the misery.

2D) He paraded the guts of sacrificed children in golden bowls and examined them so he could see into the future.

3E) He slipped bears and wild cats into guests' bedrooms as they slept.

4B) He played games where prizes were gold or lettuce leaves, diamonds or scorpions.

5C) He rewarded some dancing girls with dead dogs hung around their necks.

6J) He ordered a slave to collect 500 kilos of spiders' webs – the slave failed and was eaten alive by starving rats.

7A) He had a trick ceiling in his dining room. It opened up to flood the room with rose and violet petals – but these suffocated the guests.

8G) He gathered crowds to watch a show – then scattered poisonous snakes so that people would be bitten or trampled in the panic.

9F) The young 'god' invited friends to dinner and made them wrestle with lions and eat live parrots.

10I) His enemies were tied to a wall so he could stab them with red-hot pokers. Strips of skin were torn off them before they were dipped in salty water.

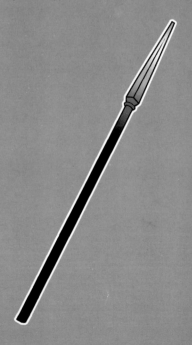

TAMERLANE THE GREAT

Mongol warrior (1336–1405)

His **savage** story

✸ Tamerlane himself was meant to be a ruthless ruler from the second he was born. How did his family know? Because baby Tamerlane was born with blood-filled hands. A deadly sign. A blood clot in the cot! Sure enough his hands were steeped in blood for the rest of his life.

✸ When he was just eight his family were taken prisoners by a Mongol army. He learned to be a robber but was shot by a shepherd when he tried to steal a sheep. The arrow wound left him with a lame leg ... and a thirst for revenge.

His **wicked** ways

✸ He executed 100,000 prisoners because it was too much trouble to guard them and feed them. His favourite building was a tower made from the 100,000 skulls of his victims. All right if you have a head for heights. Skull ... head ... geddit? Oh, never mind. The bodies were left as food for the wild animals.

✸ Tamerlane died in a freezing winter war. His tomb says:

WHEN I RISE FROM THE DEAD, THE WORLD SHALL TREMBLE.

We're still waiting.

TAMERLANE THE GREAT

TOP 50

IVAN THE TERRIBLE

His **savage** story

🟤 Ivan began ruling at the age of three and was terrible even when he was a kid. His hobby was torturing animals and he liked throwing dogs off the roof of the Kremlin palace.

🟤 His mother, who helped the kid rule, was poisoned when he was just eight. Did Ivan have mum murdered?

His **wicked** ways

🟤 Ivan's enemy, Prince Boris Telupa, had a wooden pole driven into his body and hoisted up – he took 15 hours to die, talking all the while to his mother who had been forced to watch. His minister Founilov was dipped in boiling water then had cold water poured over him so his skin peeled off like a tomato. His enemy Prince Michael was accused of being a witch and sent to be burned. Ivan shovelled hot ashes from the fire over the dying man.

🟤 Ivan carried a wooden pole with a metal spike on to lash out at people who annoyed him. One day he lashed out at his own heir and killed him.

> THAT'S LIFE ... HEIR TODAY AND GONE TOMORROW

16

JULIUS CAESAR OF AUSTRIA

Austrian nobleman (1585–1609)

His **savage** story

🌸 Julius started young … attacking servants with a knife. One servant died. His dad had him locked away for a while … good servants are hard to find. When Julius was released a lot of the other servants ran away.

🌸 Julius didn't get any better. He attacked his girlfriend, Markéta, with a knife and thought he'd killed her, so he threw her out of his castle window. She landed in the castle rubbish heap, which saved her life.

🌸 When the girl returned, Julius went mad. He… stabbed her, cut off her ears, gouged out one eye, smashed her teeth, split her skull, threw pieces of her flesh all around the room. She died.

🌸 After three hours Julius recovered from his frenzy and ordered that her body be wrapped in linen and carried away. He gave himself the job of nailing down the lid of her coffin.

His **wicked** ways

🌸 Julius was never punished because he was the son of the Emperor. After murdering Markéta he refused to wash, shave or change clothes and also refused food.

🌸 Towards the end of his life he lived in incredible filth and rubbish. He slept on carpets and when he felt cold he covered himself with what once used to be his clothes. The servants were so scared of him that no one entered his room … and also because of the terrible smell.

MURAD IV

Ruler of the Ottoman Empire (1612–1640)

His **savage** story

Murad IV of Turkey was five years old when his father died. Six years later he took the throne from his potty uncle, Mad Mustapha.

His **wicked** ways

Here are **10 foul facts** about Murad ... but ONE of them is a lie! Which one?

1. Eleven-year-old Murad hated his Grand Vezir (what we'd call a Prime Minister) and had him executed.

2. THEN Murad wanted the Vezir's friends killed. All 500 of them. They were strangled.

3. His guards set off round Baghdad, looking for spies, and Murad said, 'If you find one, kill him – or her. No trial. Find and kill.'

4. He gave his history teacher detention – hanging him in a cage without food and water till he died.

5. He ordered his guards to kill his brother.

6. He fought endless wars. In Baghdad in 1638 his men massacred 30,000 soldiers and then 30,000 women and children inside the city.

7. Murad's musician was executed for playing a song from Persia – the enemy.

8. He banned smoking, booze and coffee. The punishment was death.

9. He once came across a group of women singing in a meadow and having a picnic. 'I hate that noise,' he said. 'Drown them in the river.'

10. At night he wandered the streets in his nightshirt and killed anyone he saw. He really liked chopping the heads off men with fat necks.

Answer: Fact 4 is false. Yes, it's a nice idea ... but it didn't happen.

20

MURAD IV

TOP
50

CAPTAIN RICHARD DUDLEY

English highwayman (1681–1708)

How on EARTH do you start being a villain? Richard Dudley would tell you...

1. I WAS NINE YEARS OLD WHEN I ROBBED MY SISTER OF 30 SHILLINGS AND RAN AWAY FROM HOME.

2. I WAS SENT BACK TO SCHOOL BUT THEN STOLE MONEY FROM MY FATHER.

3. AS A TEENAGER I JOINED A GANG AND HELPED THEM IN ROBBING A COUNTRY HOUSE.

4. I WAS ARRESTED AND SENTENCED TO DEATH BUT GOOD OLD DAD GOT ME A PARDON FROM THE QUEEN.

5. AFTER A TIME IN THE ARMY AND GETTING MARRIED, I BEGAN HIGHWAY ROBBERY. WOULD YOU BELIEVE IT? I WAS ARRESTED AND SENTENCED TO DEATH AGAIN!

6. GOOD OLD DAD GOT THE SENTENCE CHANGED SO I WAS TRANSPORTED TO BARBADOS. BUT I ESCAPED FROM THE SHIP AND WENT BACK TO HIGHWAY ROBBERY.

7. I WAS CAUGHT AND SENTENCED TO DEATH WITH MY BROTHER WILL. THIRD TIME UNLUCKY, EH?

8. WILL AND I WERE HANGED. DAD CAME AND SAW US IN OUR COFFINS ... THEN DROPPED DOWN DEAD WITH THE SHOCK. GOOD OLD DAD. WAS BURIED WITH US.

Cosy, eh?

CAPTAIN RICHARD DUDLEY

TOP
50

BILLY THE KID

American outlaw (1859–1881)

His **savage** story

🌑 William Bonney (or Billy the Kid) really was a kid when he went to the pub with his mum aged 12.

🌑 A man in the bar insulted Billy's mum ... probably said, 'Mrs Bonney? You're as bonny as a baboon's bottom.'

🌑 12-year-old Billy drew a knife and stabbed the man to death.

His **wicked** ways

🌑 Billy had a friend called Pat Garrett. Pat Garrett was made sheriff of Lincoln County and had the job of hunting down Billy. Billy was caught and sentenced to hang for killing Sheriff Brady.

🌑 Billy killed his prison guards and escaped. Pal Pat tracked him down and before you could say, 'Hello, old mate,' he shot Billy the Kid dead. No more escapes.

🌑 Billy had 19 notches on his gun – one for every man he'd killed.

WANTED

· BILLY THE KID ·

KNOWN TO HAVE KILLED SHERIFF JAMES BRADY

GUILTY OF *Who was a crook and deserved it!*

CATTLE RUSTLING, ROBBERY AND MURDER

SLIM, 5 FOOT 8 INCHES. ENJOYS DANCING *sure do!*

<u>Vicious Villain</u>
<u>Tip 2</u>

If you had a dead body in the late 1700s you could sell it to doctors. They needed bodies to experiment on to find out how humans work. They were allowed to experiment on dead criminals, but not on ordinary people like you or me.

If you were a villain and you DIDN'T have a dead body then all you had to do was grab one from a grave. (Make sure it's a nice fresh one!) This was against the law ... but it made you good money. Here's a top tip from the best bodysnatchers...

1 Do NOT uncover the whole coffin. It's hard work and it takes time - you may get caught.

2 Uncover the top HALF of the coffin. Smash in the coffin lid.

3 Loop a rope under the corpse's arms and pull it out.

4 Stick it in a barrow and run to the doctor's.

KILLER CONQUERORS

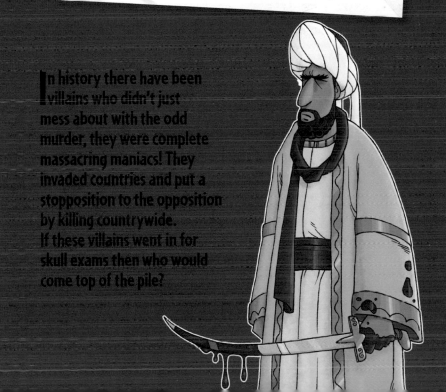

In history there have been villains who didn't just mess about with the odd murder, they were complete massacring maniacs! They invaded countries and put a stopposition to the opposition by killing countrywide.
If these villains went in for skull exams then who would come top of the pile?

ATTILA THE HUN

Leader of the Huns (AD 406–453)

His **savage** story

🔹 Attila was just 140 cm tall but a tiny terror. He smashed the Romans and anyone else who got in his way.

🔹 He massacred a city full of people to teach his enemies a lesson. Terrible tales were told of him eating human flesh.

🔹 He used attack-dogs to tear enemy armies apart.

His **wicked** ways

🔹 He wrecked the graveyards of his dead enemies.

🔹 But the most gruesome was the story that his wife, Gudrun, was even crazier than him. At a feast she served him with the hearts of their two sons Erp and Eitil for dinner. A poet described the scene ...

GUDRUN WENT OUT TO ATTILA WITH A GOLDEN CUP AND SAID, 'YOUR HIGHNESS, YOU HAVE CHEWED THE BLOODY HEARTS OF YOUR SONS, ROASTED WITH HONEY; YOU MAY DIGEST THEM, BRAVE ONE! A MEAL OF SLAIN SONS, TO EAT AS FEAST-FOOD. YOU CANNOT CALL FOR ERP NOR EITIL; YOU SHALL NOT SEE THEM AMONG THE SEATS GIVING OUT GOLD, SMOOTHING SPEAR-SHAFTS, TRIMMING MANES NOR DRIVING ON HORSES.'

There was uproar among the warriors, there was a furious song, the Huns' children wept, but Gudrun never cried for her sweet, murdered children.

🔹 What could stop awful Attila and his horrible Huns? A nosebleed. His nose started to bleed and he choked to death on his own blood.

28

ABŪ AL-ʿABBĀS AS-SAFFĀḤ

Mesopotamian ruler (722–754)

His **savage** story

★ His nickname was 'Shedder of Blood'.

★ He invited his enemies, the Umayyad family, to dinner. He had them clubbed to death, then went on with dinner – over their dead bodies.

★ He died from the disease smallpox.

His **wicked** ways

★ He also dug up the corpses of dead enemies.

★ He had the corpses flogged.

★ The dead enemies were then scattered to be eaten by wild animals. Tasty treats.

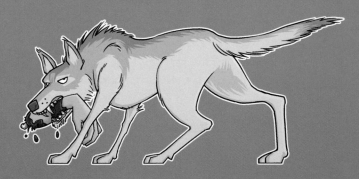

ABŪ AL-'ABBĀS AS-SAFFĀḤ

TOP 50

GENGHIS KHAN

Mongol warrior (1162–1227)

His **savage** story

❀ Ruthless raider. Genghis had a nice motto you might like to follow: 'The defeated must die so the winners may be happy.'
In other words, 'I'm not murdering you because I'm nasty – I'm doing it because it will make me happy'.

❀ In the town of Merv, Khan ordered his army to kill a million people … in a single day.

❀ By 1227 Khan was dead. Some say he fell off his horse. Others say a princess stabbed him. She must have been a ruthless royal and a strong one too.

His **wicked** ways

❀ It was said Khan was hunting with his brother when they argued about a dead bird. Khan killed his brother. He was not merciful to his enemies either – a beaten leader was strangled to death.

❀ An old woman in a defeated city tried to save her own life by promising the Mongol a pearl that she had swallowed. A soldier killed her and cut her open to get the pearl – quicker than waiting for her to poo. His leader, Genghis Khan then ordered all the prisoners' corpses be cut open in search of treasure.

❀ Khan's Mongols were starving at the siege of Beijing in 1214. Disease killed thousands of men. It was said that they ate the corpses.

VLAD THE IMPALER

Ruler of Wallachia (1431–1476)

His **savage** story

🌸 The real 'Count Dracula' was even more vicious than the vampire in the stories. Vlad used to take his prisoners of war and stick each of them on top of a sharpened pole.

🌸 The poles were then arranged around his camp and he enjoyed a tasty dinner while the victims screamed and died all around him. Something to liven up school dinners, perhaps?

His **wicked** ways

🌸 One of his nastiest tricks was to capture a group of prisoners of war. He had three of them fried alive. Their friends were then forced to eat them.

🌸 Prince Vlad had a lot of sick people in his country. They had deadly diseases like leprosy or plague. They were too sick to fight, yet Vlad could still use them in his country's fight against the Turkish invaders. The lepers and plague victims were dressed as Turks and sent to live in the Turkish army camps. The Turks would then catch the diseases and die.

🌸 Vlad became known as 'The Impaler' because he 'impaled' prisoners on the sharp poles. His other nickname was 'Dracula' … the Dragon. He didn't flit around in the shape of a bat and he didn't suck blood from innocent travellers' necks. But Dracula is the number one horror movie star.

PACHACUTI

Incan emperor (1438–1471)

His **savage** story

✸ Pachacuti's name meant 'he who shakes the Earth'. And he shook the Chanca tribes in Peru with his cruelty.

✸ When Pachacuti's kid brother became too powerful, Pachacuti had him murdered.

✸ His warriors went into battle with this cheerful song about 'chicha' beer...

WE'LL DRINK CHICHA FROM YOUR SKULL
FROM YOUR TEETH WE'LL MAKE A NECKLACE
FROM YOUR BONES WE'LL MAKE OUR FLUTES
FROM YOUR SKIN WE'LL MAKE A DRUM
AND THEN WE'LL DANCE.

His **wicked** ways

✸ The Incan emperor took the defeated Chanca leaders and stuffed their skins with straw and ashes. The scarecrow corpses were taken to a special burial ground and seated on stone benches. The stuffed arms were bent so that when the wind blew, the dead fingers beat the stretched skin on their bellies like drums.

✸ A story said that Emperor Pachacuti massacred the Chanca enemies when rocks in the hills turned into Incan warriors. But ... the truth was probably that as the Chanca ran away, hundreds of Incan supporters, living in the hills, ran down and attacked them. But Pachacuti spread the story of the warrior rocks and became one of the Inca's greatest emperors.

PACHACUTI

TOP
50

FRANCISCO SOLANO LÓPEZ

Paraguayan leader (died 1870)

His **savage** story

✺ López saw himself as the 'Napoleon' of South America and even walked around with a hand stuck in his jacket the way the French Emperor Napoleon used to do.

✺ He was so afraid of being assassinated by rebels in his army that he organised a spying system. One soldier in every three was given the job of spying on his comrades. That spy had the power to shoot anyone, including officers, who showed signs of betraying López.

✺ You'll be pleased to know the fat and foolish dictator died horribly on the end of an enemy spear – harpooned like a whale.

His **wicked** ways

✺ López sent his armies into hopeless battles where they were wiped out. So many died there were just 221,000 people left in Paraguay out of 1,337,000 when López came into power.

✺ In fact his army was really loyal. A Colonel Martinez was upset because he thought he had let López down. He decided to shoot himself in the head – but missed and shot one eye out instead. Still he went on to hold back the invaders and escape through jungles and swamps to warn his leader.

✺ How did López reward this loyal man? He had him tortured and shot for failing – and his family died the same way.

FRANCISCO SOLANO LÓPEZ

TOP 50

LEOPOLD II
King of Belgium (1835–1909)

His **savage** story

❋ This ruthless ruler was only interested in making money from his African colonies. He used ruthless soldiers to do his work. One of Leopold's men shot a native for fun. He had the dead African's head packed in a box of salt and returned to London to be stuffed and mounted in a glass case.

❋ King Leopold's soldiers ruled the Africans through terror and bullying. They sliced off the noses, ears and hands of rebels and shot women and babies. Never mind, it all went to make Leo the richest man in the world.

❋ A British explorer who passed through Leopold's African colony in 1895 reported that many African men, women and children had been brought to Stanley Falls and beheaded. Their heads had been used by Captain Rom (of the police force) as a decoration around his flowerbeds in front of his house.

His **wicked** ways

❋ King Leopold told the world he was setting the Africans free from Arab slavers. In fact working for this Belgian boss was worse than slavery. Men, women and children had to carry huge loads for their white masters – a seven-year-old child would have to carry 10-kilo loads all day through the steaming jungles. They were fed on a handful of rice and stinking dried fish. A visitor reported ...

I WATCHED A FILE OF POOR DEVILS, CHAINED BY THE NECK. THERE WERE ABOUT A HUNDRED OF THEM TREMBLING AND FEARFUL BEFORE THE OVERSEER, WHO STROLLED BY WHIRLING A WHIP. FOR EACH STRONG, HEALTHY FELLOW THERE WERE MANY SKELETONS DRIED UP LIKE MUMMIES, THEIR SKIN WORN OUT, DAMAGED BY DEEP SCARS, COVERED WITH BLEEDING WOUNDS. NO MATTER HOW FIT THEY WERE, THEY ALL HAD TO GET ON WITH THE JOB. THEY WERE BEASTS OF BURDEN WITH MONKEY LEGS.

❀ The Africans of the Congo had to produce enough rubber for Leopold's bosses on the rubber farms – or face the chicotte. What's that? It's a special, cruel whip. The sharp edges meant the whip cut into the victim's skin. A few blows would leave you scarred for life, 25 lashes could knock you out, 100 or more (quite common) would often kill you. Finally the sufferer was expected to pick himself (or herself) up and give a military salute.

❀ You don't want to work on the rubber farm? Fine … Leopold's men would hold your wife and children prisoner until you do. Or, even nastier, those children could be thrown into the jungle and left to be eaten by the animals. Or thrown onto the plains to be baked to death by the scorching sun.

JOSEPH STALIN

Russian leader (1879–1953)

His **savage** story

🍀 Leon Trotsky was one of the leaders of the 1917 Russian Revolution. Then he lost the struggle for power with the new Russian leader Joseph Stalin. Leon knew his old friend Joe would have him killed, so he ran off to hide in Mexico.

🍀 Joe Stalin's secret police were on his tail and one by one his friends and family were murdered. Leon turned his Mexican house into a fortress and survived another twelve years. On 21 August 1940 he had a young visitor – his last visitor – Ramón Mercader. Trotsky was heavily guarded but a guard let this friendly assassin through. The killer stuck an ice-pick into Trotsky's head and killed him. Stalin ruled.

🍀 Trotsky wasn't the last to die by Stalin's orders. Stalin was probably to blame for the deaths of 50 million people – most of them the Russian people on his side.

His **wicked** ways

🍀 Stalin's secret police and army wiped out anyone who stood in his way. But he helped Britain and her allies to win World War Two so no one said too much about his nasty little life. 'Winners' get away with it.

🍀 From 1934 to 1938 alone at least 7 million people 'disappeared' in Stalin's murder spree. He always said, of course, that they were criminals and their deaths were their punishment. Some of the trials were a joke. That probably makes him the greatest killer in all history.

ADOLF HITLER

German leader
(1889–1945)

His savage story

✦ Germany was in a mess after losing World War One and people wanted a strong man to lead them. Hitler had potty ideas but the Germans believed him.

✦ Private Henry Tandy was in the British Army fighting in World War One. He set off to attack a German trench. Suddenly a wounded German soldier limped out of the enemy trench and into Private Tandy's line of fire. The exhausted German never raised his rifle and just stared at Tandy waiting to be shot. Tandy said ...

The young German soldier nodded in thanks and ran off to safety. If Tandy had moved his finger a centimetre and pulled the trigger the German would have died and history would have changed. The German soldier's name was Adolf Hitler.

His wicked ways

✦ Hitler said the Jews were to blame for Germany's defeat. People believed him. He said the answer was to massacre the Jews. On 9 November 1938 Hitler sent his stormtroopers to punish the Jews. The bullies ...

✦ Smashed the windows of Jewish shops, homes and synagogues. That's why it is known as 'Kristallnacht' (crystal night) – the Night of Broken Glass.

I TOOK AIM BUT COULDN'T SHOOT A WOUNDED MAN SO I LET HIM GO.

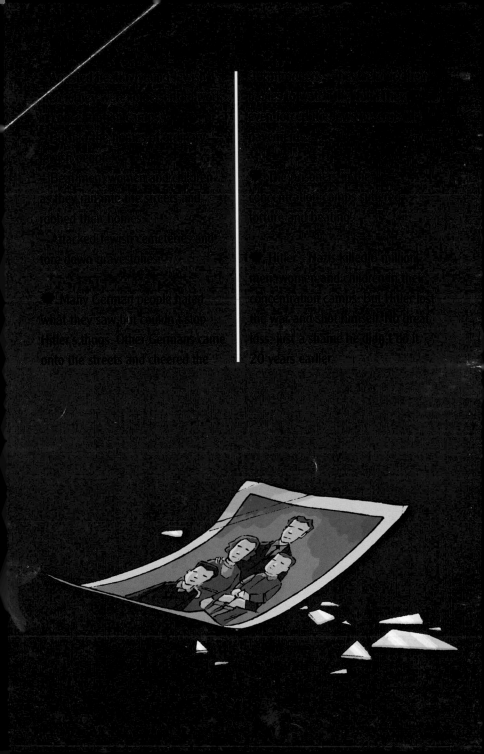

...the shops and businesses...
...other Jews. They broke into...
...Jewish homes and threw...
...out of windows.

● Beat men, women and children as they ran into the streets and robbed their homes.

● Attacked Jews in concentrated and tore down gravestones.

● Many German people hated what they saw but dared to stop Hitler's thugs. Other Germans came onto the streets and cheered the

...women...
...were forced to...
...concentration camps...

● The Nazis built concentration camps – prisons for Jews and others...

● Hitler's Nazis killed six million men, women and children in the concentration camps. But Hitler lost the war and shot himself. No great loss, just a shame he didn't do it 20 years earlier.

ADOLF HITLER

TOP
50

VICIOUS VILLAINS'
TOP TEN TOOLKIT

If you want to be a villain you need some cool kit to help. Here are a few tips from history...

1. HOMEMADE ARMOUR worn by Australian outlaw Ned Kelly (1855–1880). Not only shields you from bullets but scares your victims into giving up without a fight. But Nutcase Ned FORGOT to make leg armour. So the law officers simply shot him in the shins. Result ... Kelly caught. And his armour didn't save him when they hanged him.

2. SKELETON KEYS. Useful for breaking into houses or out of jails. The villain Jack Sheppard (1702–1724) broke out of every jail they tried to keep him in and every set of chains. In the end they caught him because he was too drunk to run away.

3. POISON. A good sneaky way to get rid of people who bother you. An Arab chemist invented the deadly white powder arsenic. It became a murderer's favourite because it had little taste and could be mixed with sugar, so you could pop it in your victim's tea. And a doctor would often say the victim died naturally of 'gastric fever'!

EVIDENCE BAG
POISON

4. MASK. Highwaymen and cowboys wore handkerchiefs over their mouths to hide their faces. Of course it also makes it easy to blow your nose!

5. RACK. A machine for stretching people till they talk. It was popular with Tudor torturers. The famous plotter Guy Fawkes was stretched on the rack till his arms and legs were almost torn out. He survived – only to be hanged, drawn and quartered.

6. SKULL. Build a pyramid with them if you're Tamerlane, or they make good drinking cups for Crusader knights. Nadir Shah of Persia (1688–1747) had towers built from the skulls of his victims. In 1119 crusader Count Robert was captured in battle and taken before the atabeg (governor) of Damascus. The atabeg drew his sword and cut off Robert's head. As if that wasn't cruel enough he threw the crusader's body to the dogs but kept his skull. It was encrusted with jewels and used as a drinking cup! General Kitchener of World War One Britain also used his enemy's skull as an inkwell.

7. NOTEPAD. Kidnappers can write ransom notes and killers can write letters to the police. In 1888 Jack the Ripper wrote to the police and made fun of them. He called himself 'Jack the Ripper' but never gave his real name – that is a GOOD idea. We still don't know who he was.

PLOD

8. CAR. Great for getaways after you've robbed a bank – but it has to be faster than the cop cars. The Dillinger Gang in the USA used cars after a robbery. In 1934 they robbed a bank in one state then drove across the border into the next state. Police weren't allowed to arrest people across the border – so they just let them go!

9. FLINTLOCK PISTOL. The flintlock pistol was invented around 1638 and was great for highwaymen. Now they had a weapon they could hold in one hand while they held their horse's reins in the other. Highwaymen were a terror on the roads from the 1600s when they robbed coaches. They disappeared in Victorian times when trains were invented. Trains are harder to catch – especially on a horse.

10. CAMERA. Take your photo if you want to be a famous villain. Send it to the papers. American gangsters like Bonnie and Clyde and John Dillinger were popular because they had their pictures taken and the public loved it. Mind you, they still ended up very dead.

Vicious Villain
Tip 3

Escape trick

On 9 Jan 1838 a scary article appeared in *The Times* newspaper:

SPRING-HEELED JACK STRIKES

It seems that a gentlemen made a bet with one of his friends. He bet he would visit London houses in three disguises - a ghost, a bear and a devil.
He would enter gardens and frighten the people of the house. This villain has already driven seven ladies out of their senses.
This joker would usually pick on women and would tear at their clothes with claws before escaping. He had a trick of breathing blue flames from his mouth as he attacked. But Spring-heeled Jack's greatest trick was to escape by jumping over fences and walls using special boots that had springs in the heels.

GRIM GANGS

It's not a lot of fun being a lonely villain but if you get a gang of cut-throats and bullies they can do the hard work for you. Of course it doesn't always work...

EUSTACE THE MONK

French monk (1170–1217)

His **savage** story

🌸 Eustace was a French monk, but he left the monastery to kill the men who had murdered his father. He became an avenging outlaw and gathered a gang of villains around him. Eustace was a great warrior and – because he hated the French who killed his dad – fought for King John of England.

🌸 Eustace had a strange way of dealing with the victims he robbed. He asked them…

If you told the truth he let you keep it. If you lied he took everything.

His **wicked** ways

🌸 Another Eustace trick was to use disguises to escape capture or spy on his enemies. He tried… fishmonger, pastry cook, crippled beggar, leper, shepherd, peasant, pilgrim and carpenter. 'Wood' you believe it?

🌸 In 1205, Eustace switched sides and fought for France. The traitor. He became a pirate, attacking English ships. The English finally captured him in 1217 after a sea battle near the coast of Kent. Eustace was given a choice…

DO YOU WANT TO BE BEHEADED ON THE SHIP'S RAIL OR ON THE TREBUCHET?

TOUGH QUESTION. WANNA GIVE ME A FEW WEEKS TO THINK ABOUT IT? A FEW YEARS MAYBE?

Eustace was beheaded on the trebuchet.

EUSTACE THE MONK

TOP 50

FRIAR TUK

English friar (1420s)

His **savage** story

🌸 In February 1416 the counties of Surrey and Sussex were in a panic. A gang was rampaging around and killing deer in the forest.

🌸 The foresters tried to stop the gang but had their houses burned down.

🌸 The leader of the gang was a foul friar with a familiar name – Friar Tuk. Remember … a 'friar' is a travelling monk, not the man in the local fish shop who cooks your chips (he is a fryer). A friar would just travel around preaching – or in Friar Tuk's case, nicking things.

His **wicked** ways

🌸 Was this the famous Friar Tuck who later made his name as a member of Robin Hood's gang? Probably not. The Tuk character was just added to the Robin Hood stories.

🌸 Was he real? Yes. It turned out Friar Tuk was a Sussex priest and deer poacher whose real name was Richard Stafford. A 'deer' man.

🌸 In the end the law gave up trying to catch Tuk and gave him a pardon.

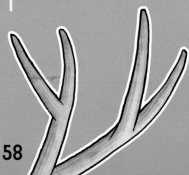

BARON BARRY OF SANTRY

Irish baron (1680–1734)

His **savage** story

🦇 Some gangs were just for foul fun. The Irish Hellfire Club was for posh young men who wanted to run wild and cruel. Men like Baron Barry of Santry. Members were known as 'Bucks'. They met at The Eagle Tavern in Dublin's city centre – how eerie is that? (Eyrie … eerie geddit? Oh, never mind.)

🦇 Sometimes they met at Montpelier Hill outside the city and away from the eyes of the Irish law. It was built in 1725. Some say the club had sacrifices. Ghostly black cats are still seen there today. Why? The black cat was their mascot. One story says a priest visited the house and saw the Hellfire Club try to sacrifice a black cat. (The priest rescued the cat you'll be pleased to hear.) Another report says they sacrificed a dwarf – but there are no ghostly dwarfs there to tell the tale.

His **wicked** ways

🦇 The members' most disgusting habit was drinking 'scultheen', a mixture of whiskey and rotten butter. Baron Barry of Santry was so drunk he stabbed one of his own servants to death. He was taken to court and sentenced to hang. But later the court decided he could live. (If the servant had stabbed the lord then you could be pretty certain he'd have hanged. If you want to get away with murder then it's better to be a baron.)

🦇 One of more gruesome Hellfire Club games was to slit open the nostrils of their victims. Why? Who nose?

JAMES DALTON

His **savage** story

🌸 Little Jim was a street robber in London. When he was five years old his dad was arrested and sentenced to hang. Mr Dalton said…

I WANT YOU TO HANG AROUND AND WATCH ME BEING EXECUTED, SON

🌸 This was to be a lesson for the boy. Young James agreed and learned … nothing really.

🌸 James went on to be a pickpocket at first.

His **wicked** ways

🌸 James Dalton joined a violent gang near St Paul's Cathedral in London. The gang smashed their way into houses and robbed people. Big mistake. Kicking doors down and sending in a mass of ruffians to rob a house was an easy crime but a shocking one. The ordinary people turned against the thugs. There was nowhere to hide.

🌸 The law officers offered a reward for their capture … When one member of the gang was arrested he made sure the others were arrested too. Dalton was furious and told the judge … 'You believe HIM? He's as big a villain as me.'

🌸 The gang hanged together as they had robbed together. That's the trouble with being in a gang – one gets caught and you all hang. Dalton died … but of course his dad wasn't there to watch.

'LITTLE' HARPE

Wild West outlaw (1770–1804)

Sometimes it's good to make a gang with your own family.

His **savage** story

❀ The Harpe Brothers were murderous outlaws in America. They were probably the first serial killers as we know them today. Sometime during 1797, the Harpes would begin their trail of death.

❀ The brothers fled from Knoxville, Tennessee, when they were accused of murdering a man named Johnson. His body was found in a river, ripped open and weighted with stones. This was a popular trick of the Harpes.

❀ The brothers killed at least 40 men, women and children on the Wild West frontier – usually so they could rob them.

His **wicked** ways

❀ An enemy called Stegal caught up with the killers and shot 'Big' Harpe. He cut off his head and stuck it on a pole. 'Big' Harpe had killed Stegal's wife so it was revenge. The place where this happened is still known as 'Harpe's Head.'

❀ 'Little' Harpe escaped. He teamed up with the villainous Samuel Mason (1739–1803), who robbed boats with his gang on the Mississippi River. But they had a bitter argument. 'Little' Harpe beheaded Sam Mason and used his head to claim the reward.

❀ But someone in the crowd pointed out that the man claiming the reward was 'Little' Harpe. Harpe was hanged and his head was stuck on a pole next to Mason's. Mason's head probably had a smile on it after that.

'LITTLE' HARPE

BEN HALL

Australian outlaw (1837–1865)

His **savage** story

🌟 Ben Hall is sometimes seen as the Robin Hood of Australia – an outlaw with a heart of gold. He and his merry men robbed ten coaches and never killed anyone (or so the story goes).

🌟 He joined a robber gang and stole gold from a coach but he never shot anyone. Why not? Depends who you want to believe. Friends of Ben Hall said, 'Ben killed no one because he was a gentleman.' An enemy of Ben Hall said, 'Ben killed no one because he was a terrible shot.'

His **wicked** ways

🌟 Ben's idea of a joke was to lock up a policeman in his own cells. Soon after that his gang of five became a gang of three when two were shot dead. Parliament put forward a law that would make Hall and his comrades into 'outlaws', meaning they would be 'outside the law' and could be killed by anyone at any time without warning. But that law had not been passed when the police finally met up with Hall and his partners.

🌟 The police tracked Ben to Goobang Creek and eight officers ambushed him. He told his friend… 'Shoot me dead, Billy! Don't let the cops take me alive.' We don't know if Billy did finish him off … but Ben Hall's body was found with THIRTY-SIX bullets in it. Police bullets? They can't all have been Billy's bullets, can they? Of course that law had not been passed so there was a big argument about the police shooting down a man before he'd been arrested.

BEN HALL

TOP 50

THE SUNDANCE KID

American outlaw (1867–1908)

His **savage** story

🌟 Harry Longabaugh joined 'The Wild Bunch' … the last of the American outlaw gangs. He had already served time in jail in the town of Sundance – so he got the name 'Sundance Kid'. But the gang wasn't as cheerful and harmless as it sounded. The Wild Bunch was led by Robert Leroy Parker, better known as 'Butch Cassidy'.

His **wicked** ways

🌟 The gang weren't that bright. No one in the gang knew they had a private detective in their midst – Charlie Siringo. He had joined the gang pretending to be an old, grizzled outlaw on the run for murder and had been accepted. This spy learned enough to spoil several planned robberies.

🌟 Sundance was said to be fast with a gun but never killed anyone. But his gang did. 'Wanted dead or alive' posters were posted through the land. They promised a massive $30,000 reward for the capture of the gang.

🌟 Butch and Sundance fled to South America where they robbed a silver mine in Bolivia. The army closed in on them and there was a gunfight at the cabin where Butch and Sundance were hiding. Soldiers heard a man in the cabin scream. There was a shot. The screaming stopped. A little later there was another shot. When the soldiers entered the cabin they found the two outlaws dead with lots of bullet wounds. They guessed that one had been wounded badly and his partner shot him to save him from any more pain – how kind. He then shot himself. But other stories say the pair somehow escaped to die of old age.

ARIZONA 'MA' BARKER

Gangster mother (1873–1935)

Her **savage** story

✿ A mother who has a gangster for a son may be a sad lady. But Arizona (or Arrie) Barker had FOUR gangster sons and she was proud of them. Her children Herman, Lloyd, Arthur and Fred Barker joined others to make a gang of 25.

✿ And who was the gang leader? Dear old mum, Ma Barker, of course. The first serious crime was Herman's. After a robbery he ran over a child in the getaway car. Herman's last crime was a robbery in 1927. He then crashed his car and shot himself so he wouldn't be arrested. The other sons were in jail.

✿ When Fred came out of prison the robberies started again. Fred's gang robbed banks and post offices, but then they were shown a new way to make their fortune – kidnapping. They made $3 million, although at least 10 people died. The gang became known as 'The Bloody Barkers'.

Her **wicked** ways

✿ The banks put out an unusual 'wanted' notice… the posters said, 'The banks will not pay for live bank robbers.' Butch and Sundance had been wanted 'Dead or alive'. The Barker family were wanted 'Dead or … erm … dead'.

✿ One by one the Barkers were captured, till at last just Ma and Fred were caught in their home. After a 45-minute gun battle the firing stopped. Ma and Fred were dead. Ma was still clutching her machine gun.

AL CAPONE

Chicago gangster (1899–1947)

His **savage** story

✹ In the 1920s alcohol was banned in the USA. That meant big money for the gangs who sold the illegal booze. Al Capone was America's most famous gangster in Chicago. But Capone had to protect his money with some pretty violent men. And it didn't pay to upset Big Al. One man who tried to steal Capone's business was 'Bugs' Moran. Al Capone set up a very special Valentine's Day gift for 'Bugs', then Al went on holiday to Florida.

✹ On 14 February 1929 Al Capone's gang dressed up as police and raided Bugs's hideout. As Bugs's gang put their hands in the air and threw down their guns, the fake cops machine-gunned them to death. It was known as 'The St Valentine's Day Massacre'.

✹ Bugs Moran lived. He was shocked. He said, 'That was meant to be me in there! I stopped off for a cup of coffee so I was late. I saw the police run in and I escaped with my life. But I thought it was just an ordinary raid. Only Capone kills like that.' He was right. Al Capone became 'Public Enemy Number One.'

Public Enemy
Number One

His **wicked** ways

❋ Al had been a good student at school. Then he dropped out of school at the age of 14, after being expelled for hitting a female teacher in the face. Al became a doorman at a nightclub when he was a young man. He insulted a young woman so her brother came along and slashed Capone's face. From then on Al's nickname was 'Scarface'. Better not call him that because he hated it. He told people the scar was a wound from fighting bravely in World War One. Liar.

❋ Two of Al's gangsters, Anselmi and Scalise, agreed to turn on their boss and kill him. Big Al heard about their plot and planned a suitable revenge. Capone arranged a big dinner party where Anselmi and Scalise were the main guests. Al gave a speech and talked about how important it was to be loyal to your boss. Then he had Anselmi and Scalise tied to their chairs. He took out a baseball bat and, in front of his guests, battered the heads of

the traitors till they were dead. If that's not enough to put you off you dinner, what is?

❋ The police arrested Capone for anything they could think of. Once he went for a walk and was put in prison for being a tramp. In the end the law said he had to go to prison for 11 years for not paying his taxes.

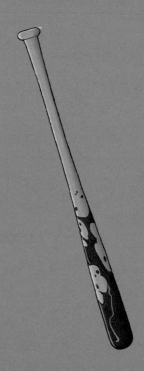

JOHN DILLINGER

American bank robber (1903–1934)

His **savage** story

✹ Dillinger was famous as the leader of an American bank-robbing gang. He started his life of crime at school where he was a bully, forever fighting. He was caught robbing a grocer's with a friend and went to prison for nearly 10 years.

✹ Dillinger was released and went straight into bank robbing. He was arrested again in 1933 and the gang showed how useful a gang can be. Three of them dressed up as prison officers, walked into the jail and set boss Dillinger free. He escaped after just four days.

✹ Then Dillinger came up with a bright new idea … well I bet YOU never thought of it … he started robbing police stations. He robbed four of them as well as 24 banks.

His **wicked** ways

✹ When Dillinger was arrested again after a bank robbery in 1934, the police said they had him in a prison that no one could escape from. Dillinger escaped. He carved a gun out of wood and used it to threaten the guards.

✹ His next gang included the famous 'Baby Face' Nelson. Dillinger was betrayed by a girlfriend who told the police which movie theatre he was in and they were waiting for him when he came out. Dillinger pulled out a gun, the police pulled out lots of guns and the gangster died with four bullets in him.

✹ His body was put on display and 15,000 people came to see the corpse. His death marked the end of the gangster age in the USA.

Vicious Villain
Tip 4

Top con trick 1 - The invisible shell

In the 1840s the British government were always
looking for new weapons to fight their wars. Samuel
Alfred Warner (1794-1853) said he had an invisible
shell. It didn't need gunpowder. He blew up two
little ships to show how it worked ... but no one was
allowed to see how he did it.
Now YOU can see how he did it, can't you?

- Load a barrel of gunpowder onto a ship at
  1 p.m. and light a one-hour fuse
- Have the ship towed out from shore and at
  2 p.m. have everyone watch it
- Tell them you've fired your invisible shell
  then watch the ship explode

Warner asked for money to show the Navy a 'long-
range' shell - one that could wreck an enemy fort
miles away. The government gave him £2,000.
But they didn't get what they expected! It was a
hot-air balloon that carried an explosive over the
target. It was supposed to land on the ship and
go off.
It didn't. It missed ... by miles. But the government
went on believing him, and paying him, for 20 years.

TERRIBLE TORTURERS

Some of the nastiest villains seem to have enjoyed making others suffer – and for others, torturing was their full-time job. You kill someone and that's it. When they die the fun ends. But kill someone s-l-o-w-l-y and the fun goes on as long as they do.

EMPEROR TIBERIUS OF ROME

Roman emperor (42 BC–AD 37)

His **savage** story

🌑 Tiberius was a great warrior, but he was not a good emperor. He was also the grumpiest old man since God sent Noah's flood. Tiberius once said: 'I don't care if they hate me so long as they respect me.'

🌑 This bad-tempered man was easily upset. And if you upset him he'd have your ears cut off and fed to his lions.

His **wicked** ways

🌑 Tiberius discovered there was a plot against him. He destroyed the rebels. Roman historian, Tacitus (AD 56–AD 120), said: 'Tiberius ordered the death of all who were lying in prison. There lay, alone or in heaps, countless dead, of every age, the great with the humble. Relatives and friends were not allowed close to them, to weep over them, or even to look at them too long. They followed the rotting corpses, till they were dragged to the Tiber, where, floating or driven on the bank, no one dared to take them for cremation or even touch them.'

🌑 There was a punishment for any man caught going to the toilet while carrying a coin with the emperor's head on, a law against kissing and a Grinch-like law to ban the giving of gifts at New Year. Disobedience to Tiberius was often punished by having legs broken.

🌑 He became so annoyed with one of his wives that he had her put into the bathroom. The servants were ordered to turn up the heat. She was steamed to death.

EMPEROR DOMITIAN OF ROME

Roman emperor (AD 51–96)

His **savage** story

🌸 Emperor Titus said, 'When I die I want my brother Domitian to take my throne.' Then Titus died. Doctors said he died of a fever but the gossips said it was poison. Would you poison your big brother to get his fortune? (Better not answer that.)

🌸 Domitian started ruling as he meant to go on by telling everyone address him as 'Master and God'. (We've all had a teacher like that at some time.)

🌸 Daft Domitian became madder and crueller the longer he ruled. He loved to torture men to death. One of his favourite nasty tricks was to chain the victim to a wall. Then the Emperor would hold a flaming torch under the man's naughty bits before cutting them off. He then watched as the poor man bled to death.

His **wicked** ways

🌸 Domitian paid for 'games' in the Roman arenas. He would make some gladiators fight blindfolded. A 'games master' whipped warriors to make them fight harder. The master's helpers came into the arena after a fight to stop any cheating. One helper came in carrying a red-hot poker and would jab the victim with the poker to make sure he was dead.

🌸 It was said that Domitian's palace was built of marble so shiny it was like a mirror. This would enable the Emperor to have 360° vision and ensure no one could sneak up behind to stab him in the back. Ironic then that he died in the palace – stabbed from the front.

EARL GODWIN

Saxon Earl of Wessex (1001–1053)

His **savage** story

❋ Poor little Prince Alfred wanted to be king after the Danish King Cnut died in 1035. But villainous Earl Godwin, Anglo-Saxon Earl of Wessex, had other ideas. The Anglo-Saxon Chronicle reported the event but it's a bit dull to read. If the miserable monks had been potty poets it might have looked like this…

Prince Alfred was a cheerful lad,
with eyes of sparkling blue,
Till Godwin had his eyes put out,
yes both! Not one, but two!
He sent the blinded prince away
to be a monk in Ely.
There the little Alfie died;
did Godwin care? Not really.

Then Godwin set about the slaying of Alf's friends.
He had them caught and had them brought to really sticky ends.

Some he sold as slaves for cash
and some he scalped their head,
Others he locked up in chains
and some he killed stone dead.

Some he had their hands chopped
off or arms or legs or ears.
No wonder they all fled
(or tried to flee) in fear.
We've never seen a crueller deed
been done in all our land,
Since those dread Vikings came
and took peace from our hands.

His **wicked** ways

❋ The Anglo-Saxons believed that God took revenge on villains. 'An eye for an eye' the Bible said. So Alfie would be pleased to know that Godwin's son, Harold, died at the Battle of Hastings 30 years later … with an arrow in his eye!

EARL GODWIN

TOP
50

ALEXANDER STEWART

'The Wolf of Badenoch'
(1343–1405)

His **savage** story

🍀 Awful Alex ruled the north of Scotland and had a nasty habit of hunting in the Rothiemurchus Forest. He set fire to parts of it to drive out the deer and kill them. But he also enjoyed hunting outlawed men this way.

🍀 When he caught a victim he had them locked in a cellar with a metre of icy water.

🍀 If the prisoner stood up they would live – if they tried to sit down or fell asleep, they would drown. They were left there for two or three days. If they lived then they were set free.

His **wicked** ways

🍀 Alex was upset by an enemy so he destroyed the city of Elgin. His men set fire to the cathedral, the monastery of the Greyfriars, a parish church and the hospital.

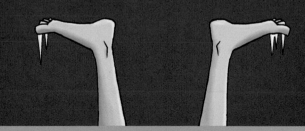

TOMÁS DE TORQUEMADA

Spanish torturer (1420–1498)

His **savage** story

✤ A Christian monk. Surely this was a peaceful enough job?

✤ No, he decided Jews were dangerous people and he would torture people to discover who were the good Christians and who were not.

✤ But how could you tell if someone was a Protestant or a Jew or a witch? They changed their underpants on Sunday. That's right. Anyone changing knickers or underpants on a Sunday could end up in a torture chamber. But how did Torquemada's spies KNOW???

His **wicked** ways

✤ The Church said Tom's torturers must not spill any of their victims' blood. So what did they do?

– Used thumbscrews to squeeze their fingernails.
– Tore their flesh with white-hot irons (to 'seal' the wound before blood could flow).
– Roasted them over fires.
– Forced water down their throats till they almost drowned.
– Hung them from the ceiling by their wrists and put weights on their feet.

✤ The ones who lived through the torture were usually burned.

TOMÁS DE TORQUEMADA

GYÖRGY DÓZSA

Hungarian rebel (1470–1514)

His **savage** story

❁ To the people, György Dózsa was a Christian hero who led the peasants, students, monks and priests against their cruel lords. To the posh Hungarians, he was a dangerous criminal.

❁ He stuck many enemies on the sharp point of a pole and let them die slowly. That led to the ancient *Horrible Histories* joke…

ALL RIGHT … I GET THE POINT!

I KNEW HE WAS GOING TO SAY THAT!

SO PREDICTABLE

❁ Sometimes György Dózsa crucified them. Thousands of those fighting for the lords died.

His **wicked** ways

❁ When he was captured you can be sure his enemies had a special treat waiting for him.

❁ He was sat on a heated iron throne with a red-hot iron crown on his head and a hot sceptre in his hand (making fun of his plans to be king).

❁ While Dózsa was suffering his younger brother, Gergely, was cut in three in front of his eyes. Dózsa was then set upon and eaten by six other rebels, who had been starved. If they ate their defeated leader they lived. If they refused they were chopped. So was Dózsa a cruel and crucifying villain? Or a victim? Or both?

RICHARD TOPCLIFFE

Elizabethan torturer (1531–1604)

His **savage** story

🌸 When Elizabeth I came to the English throne, the top torturer was Richard Topcliffe. He was made for the job because he loved giving pain to people. He boasted that his own instruments and methods were better than the ones in the Tower of London.

🌸 The Tower of London's 'rack' machine is made of pulleys and levers. It was used for stretching the person until their joints separated.

🌸 While being stretched, Topcliffe's torturers may burn the bottoms of your legs and pull out your toenails. Other prisoners may be invited to watch your suffering as it could encourage them to talk.

His **wicked** ways

🌸 A Catholic priest called Father John Gerard survived the torture of Topcliffe and lived to tell the tale. 'They took steps one by one from beneath my feet so that I hung by my hands and arms. I hung in this way till I fainted. Then the men lifted me up, or replaced those steps under my feet, until I came to myself; and immediately they heard me praying they let me down again. This they did over and over again, eight or nine times.'

🌸 Brave Gerard suffered three days of this treatment before he managed to escape from the Tower with the help of a rope.

🌸 Topcliffe died at the age of 73. Being a torturer didn't do him much harm then?

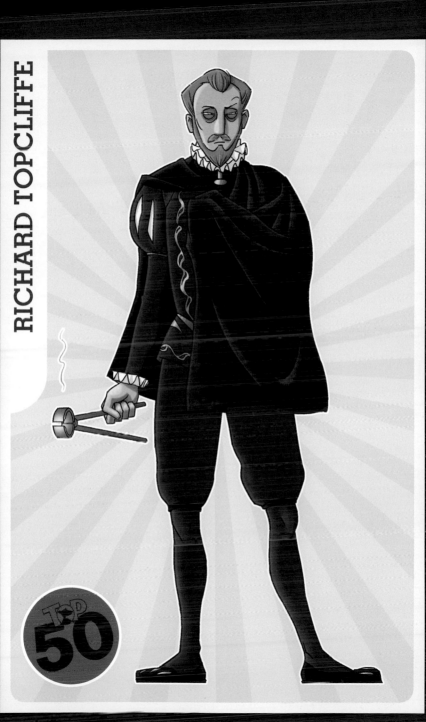

RICHARD TOPCLIFFE

TOP
50

ELIZABETH BRANCH

English murderer (1687–1740)

Her **savage** story

🌟 You don't have to be a ruler to be a torturer. Elizabeth Branch was just a rich woman – filthy rich.

🌟 Lousy Liz used to catch flies and kill them and loved to torment dogs and cats. When she married she taught her daughter Betty cruel ways. Betty often cut open live mice and birds, torturing them for three hours before they died.

🌟 Liz and Betty began tormenting the servants. One servant said the Branch family forced him to eat his own poo.

Her **wicked** ways

🌟 Another 13-year-old servant was late so the brutal Branches beat her with rods, broomsticks and shoes for seven hours ... till she died. (Then they stopped.)

🌟 At the trial Liz and Betty even managed to kick some of the witnesses.

🌟 The Branches were hanged. The people of the village hated Liz and Betty. They would have torn their bodies apart at the hanging – so the cruel couple were hanged at 6 a.m. before most people were out of bed.

EVIL ENDS

Some villains have come to very nasty ends. So, when you become a villain, how would YOU like to die? Here's your choice, from a deadly lance to barrels of wine...

SIGURD I OF ORKNEY (DIED 892)

Viking Sigurd was a cheat! He conquered and ruled Orkney well, but then he attacked Scotland and made enemies.

He told his chief enemy Maelbrigte ...

LET'S SETTLE THIS ONCE AND FOR ALL. I WILL FIGHT YOU TO THE DEATH WITH 40 HORSEMEN

I AGREE

Sigurd turned up with 40 horses ... but with two men on each horse. The Vikings won, of course. Sigurd lopped off the head of Maelbrigte, fastened it to his saddle and rode home.

But Maelbrigte had buck teeth. One of the teeth rubbed against Sigurd's leg. It made a wound which turned septic and Sigurd died of the blood poisoning.

That's the tooth, the whole tooth and nothing but the tooth.

GRAND PRINCE ÁLMOS OF HUNGARY (DIED 895)

This powerful prince rampaged around Europe and beat lots of people in battles. But he was told...

YOU WILL BE FIRST OF A LONG LINE OF GREAT KINGS BUT NEVER ENTER THE LAND OF PANNONIA

The Pecheneg people there had a habit of turning enemy skulls into drinking cups. That gives us a bit of a clue why it would be wise to keep out of their lands in Pannonia.

So Álmos went to Pannonia ... villains never learn, do they? He was defeated and sacrificed by horse. Here's how...

fig I. First take four horses and four ropes.

fig II. Tie one end of each rope to each horse and the other ends to the wrist or ankle of the villain.

fig III. Frighten the horses so they all run off in different directions.

fig IV. Pick up the bits and put them on show.

Of course that story is a bit too clever to believe. Other reports say Pedro de Valdivia...

* was beaten to death
* was pierced with a wooden stake
* had his heart cut out and eaten.

What have you got? Five bleeding villain bits.

THE DUKE OF CLARENCE (DIED 1478)

Cruel Clarence wanted the throne of England ... but his brother King Richard III stood in the way. Clarence plotted against Richard and rotten Rich found out.

It is said that Richard had Clarence drowned in a barrel of wine.

Others say the drowning is just a story. A body was dug up many years later that was probably Clarence's. It had been beheaded. A noble way to die ... so wine not?

PEDRO DE VALDIVIA (DIED 1554)

The Spanish Conquistadors smashed the natives of Peru to steal their gold. Pedro was captured and the Peruvian warriors gave him a pot of gold ... scalding, melted gold.

They poured it down his throat and said (in Incan language)...

YOU WERE THIRSTY FOR OUR GOLD, SO DRINK!

HENRY II OF FRANCE (DIED 1559)

Henry enjoyed jousting as a knight ... you know, charging at one another with lances.

But Henry was KING ... so he couldn't have a plain iron helmet, oh no. He had to have one with a golden visor to shield his face. But gold is soft (like Henry's brain).

A rival's lance splintered and smashed through the soft golden visor. The splinter went into Henry's eye and popped out of his ear. He took ten days to die, slowly and horribly.

JERRY ABERSHAW (DIED 1795)

Being a villain is no fun if you can't have a joke ... even in the bad times.

Highwayman Jerry Abershaw was sentenced to death for his crimes. He enjoyed the last couple of weeks of his life...

✸ When a judge sentenced a villain he would put on a black cap and speak these deadly words...

> "THE SENTENCE OF THE COURT UPON YOU IS, THAT YOU BE TAKEN FROM THIS PLACE TO A LAWFUL PRISON AND THENCE TO A PLACE OF EXECUTION AND THAT YOU BE THERE HANGED BY THE NECK UNTIL YOU ARE DEAD; AND THAT YOUR BODY BE AFTERWARDS BURIED WITHIN THE GROUNDS OF THE PRISON. AND MAY THE LORD HAVE MERCY ON YOUR SOUL. AMEN."

To show he didn't care, Jerry ALSO put on a black cap as the judge sentenced him. He replied...

> "AND YOU ARE A MURDERER."

✸ While Jerry waited for his execution someone sent him a bowl of cherries. He used the cherry juice to paint pictures of his crimes on the prison-cell walls.

✸ When he was taken to hang outside the prison walls he wore an open white shirt and a flower in his mouth. He joked with the crowd who'd come to see him die.

✸ The last thing he did was take off his boots! Jerry said...

> "MY MUM ALWAYS SAID I WAS SUCH A CRIMINAL I'D DIE WITH MY BOOTS ON ... WELL YOU WERE WRONG, MA!!"

Good people (like you and me) are supposed to die peacefully in bed – with our boots OFF.

DAN MORGAN (DIED 1865)

This Australian outlaw was also known as John Smith, Sydney Bill, Dan Owen, Down-the-River Jack and Billy the Native. He attacked people on the road, beat them half to death ... then sobbed, 'Forgive me! I'm sorry!' So that's all right then.

At Peechelba he went into a tavern and held all the people hostage. But one serving girl slipped out and warned the police. When Morgan came out with his hostages he was shot in the back and died six hours later.

His body was taken to Wangaratta, where a strange thing happened. The body was propped up in a stable and shown to the public. His eyes were opened and one of his pistols was put in his hand. Photographs were then taken and lumps of his hair were chopped from his head as souvenirs.

The police stopped it, but worse was to come. Morgan's head was cut off and sent to Melbourne; his headless body was buried at the Wangaratta cemetery.

GRIGORI RASPUTIN (DIED 1916)

The Mad Monk Rasputin became a great friend of the Russian royal family. He used his power to get lots of gifts and even chatted up the Queen and her daughter. The Russian nobles hated him and Prince Felix Yusupov plotted to kill him. Felix SAID...

"FIRST I GAVE HIM ENOUGH POISON TO KILL SIX MEN, BUT HE LIVED ... THEN I SHOT HIM IN THE CHEST ... BUT WHEN I WENT TO CHECK THE CORPSE HE JUMPED UP AND ATTACKED ME ... I RAN AND HE FOLLOWED. MY FRIENDS BEAT HIM SENSELESS. THEY TIED HIM INTO A CHAIR AND THREW IT IN THE FREEZING RIVER."

Fantastic Felix! BUT... every time Felix told the story he changed it. The TRUTH may be different. The body of the monk had NO poison and he HADN'T drowned. He died from a bullet in the head.

Vicious Villain
Tip 5

Top con trick 2 –
The water bottle trick

Wild West bank robber Butch Cassidy (real name Robert Leroy Parker) was born in Utah in 1866 and was robbing trains before he was 20.

In 1889, Cassidy joined Tom McCarty. Inside a bank, McCarty held up a small bottle which he said contained high explosive.

'If I drop this we'll all be blown into the next state!'

The bank gave him $21,000 to go away. As he left the bank with the cash, he threw the bottle into a waste-paper basket. It was full of water. Ho! Ho!

VICIOUS VILLAINS WITH B-I-G IDEAS

A villain may mug his granny for the 10p in her purse, but that's just a start. A real villain has B-I-G ideas and wants to smash and rob the whole world.

KING HEROD THE GREAT

King of Judea (74–4 BC)

His **savage** story

✸ Herod was King of Judea (South Palestine). He made friends with the mighty Romans and their army made Herod king. He reigned for 37 years and his last years were a reign of terror.

✸ If anyone opposed Herod then some of his 2,000 bodyguards took them away and got rid of them.

✸ He heard that a baby had been born who would become King of the Jews. He didn't know WHICH baby. So Herod decided to think BIG. 'Easy. We simply kill ALL the baby boys aged 2 or under in Bethlehem. Off you go. Chop! Chop!' (Bethlehem was a small place so 'all the boys' probably meant around 20.)

His **wicked** ways

✸ Of course the baby he was out to kill was Jesus … and Jesus escaped. (Well, he would. He had a host of angels to help him. The Bible says the Wise Men had a dream that Herod would try to kill Jesus.)

✸ You weren't even safe if you were a grown-up boy … Herod had his own sons executed as well as his wife, Mariamne. Nice Dad. Nice husband.

✸ Herod was worried that no one would cry when he died. So he ordered that a group of top men should come to Jericho … and be executed. That way there would be lots of crying families! (Herod's son, the new king, didn't carry out the executions. Herod died, no one cried.)

WU ZHAO

Empress of China (624–705)

Her **savage** story

🦴 She started out as one of the emperor's many wives. But Wu Zhao decided to think BIG. She decided she wanted to rule the whole country.

🦴 She knew she had to get rid of hubby's other wives – have them murdered or thrown into jail. So first she killed her own baby… and blamed it on Empress Wang.

🦴 The emperor believed her and let her execute the innocent empress. She had her hands and feet cut off… then had her drowned in a barrel of wine.

Her **wicked** ways

🦴 When the emperor died she had his weakest son put on the throne, then told him how she wanted the country to be run.

🦴 In the end she just took over as emperor. Easy! Just think BIG.

🦴 She ruled for 15 years. Then her son returned from abroad and threw her off the throne. She died … but she was aged 80, so she hadn't done badly.

WU ZHAO

BASIL II

His **savage** story

🌸 Basil became emperor when he was a young man and faced a rebellion from one of his generals, Skleros. Skleros was defeated but allowed to live. He ended his days blind. Maybe he had an eye disease, but knowing Basil's nasty little habits he may have been punished by blinding.

🌸 Blind Skleros gave Basil some advice...

'IF YOU WANT TO STAY IN POWER YOU NEED GOVERNORS TO HELP. BUT IF ANY OF THEM GET TOO PROUD THEN CUT THEM DOWN.'

And Basil learned that lesson well.

His **wicked** ways

🌸 In 1014 Basil's army managed to surround the enemy forces, the Bulgars, and they surrendered. Did he spare them? Not exactly.

🌸 He blinded the whole Bulgar army ... not just one or two leaders. Bas thought BIG. He blinded every enemy soldier, EXCEPT he left one eye to every 100th man, so that the other 15,000 soldiers might be led back to their king, Samuel. Sad Sam died of shock two days after seeing this terrible spectacle. The blinded Bulgar army would never go home to be teachers – no pupils, you see?

🌸 Basil got a new name, Basil Bulgaroktonus ... which means 'Slayer of the Bulgars'.

CHRISTOPHER COLUMBUS

Italian explorer (1451–1506)

His **savage** story

✤ Christopher Columbus 'discovered' America in 1492 even though it was never lost.

✤ When he set off for home he kidnapped around 20 Native Americans. The terrible conditions on the ships meant only seven arrived in Spain alive. They were enough to show the Spanish that these strong Native Americans would make great slaves.

✤ Columbus headed back to America – and this time he had over 1,200 soldiers armed with guns, swords, cannon and attack-dogs. And he wasn't going for a holiday – Disney World hadn't been invented. He was going back for more slaves.

His **wicked** ways

✤ In 1495 the Spanish rounded up 500 Arawak Indians on Haiti to be sent back to Spain and took another 500 to work for them on the islands. Half the slaves died on the journey but Cruel Chris didn't care.

✤ Forced work and dreadful diseases killed all the Arawaks off in time. Anyone who disobeyed would have his (or her) nose cut off or ears lopped. Then they were sent back to the village as a warning to the others.

✤ When they ran out of Native American slaves the Spanish started capturing them in Africa and taking them across the Atlantic to work in America. Cruel Chris began the terrible slave trade that lasted another 400 years.

CHRISTOPHER COLUMBUS

TOP
50

TIZOC

Aztec emperor (reigned 1481–1486)

His **savage** story

🔶 When Emperor Tizoc wanted a sacrifice he believed that the gods wanted 20 warriors to die on the pyramid in Tenochtitlan.

🔶 Then he decided to terrify all the other tribes in Mexico with a huge massacre. He took every single man from three Mixtec tribes – 20,000 men – and sent them for sacrifice. That's thinking BIG.

🔶 The victims had eagle feathers stuck to them with their own blood and were led to the Aztec capital. They were all killed on the pyramid. The Aztec warriors killed the first ones, then the priests took over.

His **wicked** ways

🔶 In early sacrifices the people had eaten small parts of the victims. This time there were too many. They were simply killed and their bodies thrown into the marshes.

🔶 It terrified the other tribes in Mexico all right, but it also disgusted them. They learned to hate the Aztecs. They knew they would have to wait, but one day their chance would come to overthrow the vicious heart-ripping people. And it did.

🔶 Tizoc died after reigning just five years. He was probably poisoned by his own family. The victims of his sacrifices must have fallen off the pyramid laughing.

TIZOC

TOP
50

CAPTAIN THOMAS BLOOD

Irish jewel thief (1618–1680)

His **savage** story

🔹 No one can steal the Crown Jewels from the Tower of London. They are the most closely guarded valuables in the toughest of towers.

🔹 But Irish villain Thomas Blood thought BIG. Blood made friends with the keeper of the jewels, Talbot Edwards, and got himself invited to dinner. He tied up the keeper, stuffed some jewels down his trousers and rode off. He was caught by a guard as he was almost out of the gates and free.

His **wicked** ways

🔹 Blood was taken before the King Charles II himself, who decided he liked a man with such big ideas.

Charles forgave him and gave him a pension of £500 a year. Lucky Blood.

🔹 Captain Blood had the cheek to tell the King that…

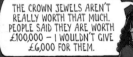

THE CROWN JEWELS AREN'T REALLY WORTH THAT MUCH. PEOPLE SAID THEY ARE WORTH £100,000 – I WOULDN'T GIVE £6,000 FOR THEM.

Charles was amused and released the thief. Why would he do that? Some people believe Charles II set up the whole thing – that he planned to steal his own jewels and sell them.

🔹 Not only did Blood get an Irish estate from Charles, he was also welcomed into the royal court where he was a popular figure. But Blood went to his grave with some vicious words on his tombstone:

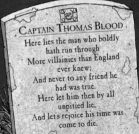

CAPTAIN THOMAS BLOOD
Here lies the man who boldly hath run through
More villainies than England ever knew;
And never to any friend he had was true.
Here let him then by all unpitied lie,
And let's rejoice his time was come to die.

CAPTAIN THOMAS BLOOD

TOP
50

Vicious Villain
Tip 6

Top charmer's tip

George Joseph Smith (1872-1915) killed three women
by drowning them in their baths. First he would trick
them into giving him all of their money and then he
would say... 'My dear, are you all right? You just
fainted!' When the victim said, 'No I didn't,' Smith
told them, 'Don't you remember? Oh, dear. It must
have been a fit.' The poor woman would think she
needed to see a doctor. After they came back from the
doctor Smith got them to take a bath. As they soaked
he pulled their ankle and pushed down on their head.
The sudden rush of water into their lungs drowned
them quickly. THEN George called the same doctor and
said, 'It must have been one of her fits! Boo! Hoo!'
The doctor agreed. Then Smith changed his name, found
another victim and so it went on. Until ... the second
woman's dad saw a report of the third victim. 'Hello,'
he said, 'That's how MY daughter died! The police
should be told!' Savage Smith was arrested and hanged.
His mistake was to try the same trick again and again.

WICKED
WOMEN

Villains have usually been men. But don't despair you female fans. Females CAN become villains too. Some women have made a really good job of it.

CLEOPATRA VII

Queen of Egypt (69–30 BC)

Her **savage** story

✸ Cleo shared the throne of Egypt with her little brother Ptolemy XIII. After she met top Roman ruler Julius Caesar she didn't need little brother – and little brother was discovered drowned.

✸ Cleopatra was interested in poisons. It's said she used to test them on prisoners in the Egyptian jails.

✸ Her Roman boyfriend Julius Caesar came to a sticky end – he was stabbed to death by the posh Romans – so Cleo moved on to Roman general Mark Antony.

Her **wicked** ways

✸ In 34 BC, Mark Antony returned with Cleopatra to Egypt. Crowds swarmed to the city to catch a glimpse of the golden couple seated on golden thrones that were raised on silver platforms.

✸ But Antony was no Caesar on the battlefield or the seas and they lost a war against Rome.

✸ The famous story is that Cleopatra killed herself, bitten by a poison snake … an asp. It's tricky killing yourself that way. BUT… No one wrote about Cleo's death at the time it happened. The story of the asp was written a hundred years after she died. Maybe Cleo DIDN'T kill herself – maybe she was murdered by her enemies.

116

CLEOPATRA VII

TOP
50

LUCREZIA BORGIA

Italian duchess (1480–1519)

Her **savage** story

☠ Lucrezia is supposed to be one of the deadliest women ever to have lived.

☠ It is SAID that Lucrezia wore a ring that was filled with poison. Her husband's enemies were invited to a meeting and she served them wine – then slipped in the poison. When adults drink wine they clink their glasses together. That is said to be an idea from the days of the Borgias. If a little wine slops from each glass to the other, it proves the other person hasn't put poison in yours.

Her **wicked** ways

☠ Some historians think tales of lousy Lucrezia may not be true – they were mostly lies made up by the Borgias' enemies.

☠ Lucrezia's whole family were dangerous people.

☠ Her brother Cesare Borgia and their father, Pope Alexander VI, enjoyed stabbing, shooting at passers-by with a crossbow, strangling, and … most of all … poisoning.

MARY TUDOR

Queen of England (1516–1558)

Her **savage** story

🟐 Henry VIII's daughter didn't manage to kill as many people as her dad, but that's because she didn't reign as long.

🟐 Mary threatened to kill her own sister, Elizabeth, because she thought she was plotting against her.

🟐 Henry VIII made England follow the Protestant religion. Mary took the throne and said everyone had to go back to being Catholic. The ones who refused were executed horribly. They were tied to a stake and burned.

Her **wicked** ways

🟐 Some modern historians think Mary has been treated unfairly in history books. 'She wasn't all that bad,' they say. In terms of executing people her father Henry VIII was worse.

🟐 It's the horrible burnings where she's the Top Tudor with a nasty habit of burning Protestants. See how they compare below:

Terrible Tudor	Rotten Reign	Burned	Awful Average
Mary	4 years	300	75 each year
Henry VIII	38 years	81	2 each year
Henry VII	24 years	10	One every 2 years
Elizabeth	45 years	5	One every 9 years

🟐 Mary aimed to be kind by allowing the executioner to strap gunpowder to her victim's legs so they'd go with a quick 'spark-bang-splatter'. But it often didn't work. More 'spark-splutter-sizzle'.

120

MARY TUDOR

TOP
50

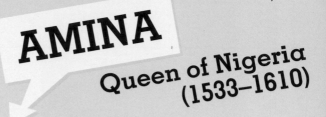

AMINA
Queen of Nigeria
(1533–1610)

Her **savage** story

✤ This warrior queen changed the history of Nigeria.

✤ She started training to fight at 16 and went on fighting until her death nearly 60 years later.

✤ She made the roads safe for her traders and built massive forts for her people. Awesome Amina. Not a villain at all…

Her **wicked** ways

✤ …except for one nasty little habit. Because she was busy making war she had no time for a full-time husband.

✤ She never married. But wherever she went and conquered, she chose a 'boyfriend' from the captured enemy.

✤ He got a lovely cuddle all night long, but little did he know Amina would have him killed the next morning.

JOAN FLOWER

Witch of Belvoir (died 1619)

Her **savage** story

🌸 Witches were often said to work in gangs... except they called them 'covens'. They BELIEVED they could perform spells, but we know it was nonsense.

🌸 The Witches of Belvoir were said to be magical murderers. Joan Flower and her daughters Margaret and Philippa were sacked from their jobs as servants for the Earl of Rutland. They were accused of pinching stuff.

Her **wicked** ways

🌸 Joan planned revenge...

'FIRST WE TAKE THESE STOLEN GLOVES FROM THE EARL'S SON, HENRY – STICK PINS IN AND DROP THEM IN BOILING WATER...'

Henry died a week later.

🌸 The mad mum wasn't happy with one death. She said ...

'NOW WE TAKE THESE STOLEN GLOVES FROM THE EARL'S OTHER SON, FRANCIS – AND BURY THEM IN A TOILET PIT.'

In weeks, young Francis was also dead. The three Flowers and three witch friends were arrested. Joan said,

'GIVE ME BREAD. IF I AM A WITCH I WILL CHOKE ON IT.'

They gave her the bread ... and she choked to death.

🌸 The remaining women then turned on each other. (That's the problem with being in a gang – if one's in trouble they're all in trouble.) They were all hanged at Lincoln Prison on 11 March 1619.

HANNAH DAGOE

Irish thief (died 1763)

Her **savage** story

🌸 This heartless thief broke into Widow Hussey's room and stripped it of everything the poor woman owned.

🌸 Hannah was sentenced to be hanged, but she didn't go quietly on the hanging cart.

🌸 The big, tough woman struggled to get her arms free and attacked her executioner, Thomas Turlis. She said…

I DARE YOU TO TRY AND HANG ME!

Her **wicked** ways

🌸 She punched the executioner so hard in the chest that she flattened him. She then threw her hat, cloak and other articles of clothing into the crowd, so the hangman couldn't sell them.

🌸 At last she was overpowered and Turlis got the rope around her neck.

🌸 But before the signal was given for the cart to move off, Hannah bound a handkerchief around her own head and over her face. Then she threw herself out of the cart with such force that she broke her neck and died at once.

RANAVALONA I

Queen of Madagascar (reigned 1828–1861)

Her **savage** story

✿ Ranavalona had cruel eyes like a snake. She started acting evil at a very early age ... then got worse.

✿ She married King Radama I when she was very young and poisoned him. Ranavalona took the throne after bumping off any rivals. She then had most of her family assassinated.

✿ She hated foreigners, especially the island's Christian missionaries, and drove them out. But many of her own people stayed Christian and needed to be dealt with. They were dangled over a 50-metre cliff by a rope, then asked, 'Do you worship the Queen's god or Christ?' If they answered, 'Christ,' the rope was cut.

Her **wicked** ways

✿ Anyone who owned a Bible was executed. Some victims were tied up like chickens and thrown from hilltops. If that didn't kill them they were thrown again ... and again ... until they did die.

✿ Some were yoked together like cattle and left in the tangled jungles of Madagascar where they would break their necks trying to get free, or would get caught in the undergrowth and starve to death.

✿ But Ranavalona's favourite method of execution was to have a prisoner dropped in a pit at the bottom of a hill. Her soldiers, at the top of the hill, would tip over pots of boiling water; when the water reached the pit, it would slowly rise up and boil the prisoner alive.

128

MARY ANN COTTON

English killer (1832–1873)

Her **savage** story

🌑 Misery Mary of County Durham in England killed about 15 of her own children and three husbands. She fed the children with a poison called arsenic from a teapot.

🌑 They died a slow and painful death. She tried to have her last child taken into a workhouse but the workhouse refused to take the boy. Mary said… 'Never mind … he won't grow up.' The workhouse keeper said, 'He looks a healthy lad to me!' A week later the boy was dead.

Her **wicked** ways

🌑 Mary was arrested and hanged. The police found out about all the people who had died in her 'care' – husbands and children mainly.

🌑 She killed most of them with arsenic. The careless doctors said they had all died from stomach upsets.

🌑 A hundred years later Durham children still sang this skipping song:

MARY ANN COTTON, SHE'S DEAD AND SHE'S ROTTEN,
SHE LIES ON HER BED WITH HER EYES WIDE OPEN.
SING, SING! WHAT SHALL I SING?
MARY ANN COTTON IS TIED UP WITH STRING.
WHERE, WHERE? UP IN THE AIR,
SELLING BLACK PUDDINGS A PENNY A PAIR.

🌑 Black puddings? They are swollen tubes of blood … like the legs of a hanged woman. Nasty song for a nasty woman.

MARY ANN COTTON

TOP
50

ALICE HOLT

Arsenic poisoner (died 1863)

Alice Holt poisoned her mother with arsenic and a poem of the time told the tale...

A dreadful case of poison,
such as we seldom hear,
Committed was at Stockport,
in the county of Cheshire.
Where a mother named Mary Bailey,
they did so cruelly slaughter,
By poison administer all in her beer,
by her own daughter.
She made a plan to murder her,
as we now see so clear,
To put a quantity of arsenic
into her poor mother's beer.

But there's no doubt the base wretch
did her poor mother slay,
For which on Chester scaffold
her life did forfeit pay.
So all young women a warning take,
by this poor wretch you see,
A-hanging for her mother's sake
on Chester's fatal tree.

What a crime ... against poetry!

Vicious Villain
Tip 7

Top con trick 3 - Tricking the greedy

Promise to make people rich. Sell them a brilliant
idea. Get them to pay you ... then disappear with
the money and the secret.

Henry Ford made a fortune from his company - the
Ford Motor Company. But still he wanted more money.
One day he received a letter from a stranger called
Professor Enricht. Enricht said he had a special
mixture which could make cars run on water! All
Ford had to do was pay him $100,000 now and the
rest when he'd sold the mix to the world. He had
nothing to lose! Henry Ford saw a car run on a
bucket of water ... with a magic liquid added. He
paid $10,000 for the secret. Enricht then sent the
same letter to a gun-maker, Hiram Maxim. Maxim said
he'd give Enricht $100,000. Enricht took the Maxim
money, handed over an envelope and told Maxim not
to open it till Enricht said he could. Then Enricht
disappeared. Maxim opened the envelope. It was full
of blank paper.

THE GOOD VILLAIN

Can you be a 'good' villain? Some people think it's OK to rob the rich if you give the loot to the poor. The most famous good villain is Robin Hood of course.

ROBIN HOOD

English outlaw (around 1200)

🌸 Records show that a man with a name like Robin Hood lived in Wakefield, England. If you want to see where the 'Real' Robin Hood lived, go to Wakefield Bus Station – his house was somewhere underneath the bus stop ... maybe.

🌸 The story says Robin fought for his king, Edward II. When the King was thrown off the throne Rob had to hide in Barnsdale Forest. Lots of stories were told about this outlaw. But his death is a real warning that says 'trust nobody'.

🌸 Robin grew old and sickly from all that living in the forest and turned to a relation for help, his cousin Elizabeth de Staynton, who was a naughty nun. The tales of Robin Hood were told at first as poems. They are in Old English and hard to follow. Here's a new version...

Robin grew quite old and grey,
Long past robbing rich (they say).
He said, 'I don't feel very good ...
It's all that living in the wood ...
... Bad for a wrinklie like me!

'To Kirklees Abbey I'll be buzzin'
The Prioress there she's my cousin.
My cousin Beth is the top nun
She'll feed me up with cakes and buns ...
... And maybe a nice cup of tea.'

Now Robin had an ene-mee
Called Roger of old Donkes-lee.
Rob doesn't know the man he hates
With good old Beth was best of mates ...
... and she fancied him too.

So Rob arrived and Prioress said,
'Just lie down, Rob, upon this bed.
The problem is, dear Robin Hood,
You're full of too much real bad blood ...
... so we'll let some out.'

But that bad nun she played a trick,
She took a knife and made a nick.
He thought he'd lose a little blood
Instead she let out quite a flood ...
... and finished him off.

And so he died in pools of red
And all the poor men wept (it's said).
So don't go trusting nuns called Beth
Or they may bring about your death ...
... or worse.

DID YOU KNOW...?

Robin's favourite Merry Man was Little John. But
not many people know Little John used to work for
Rob's enemy the Sheriff of Nottingham. Then one day
a servant was slow to serve Little John - John went
off in a huff and joined Robin's gang. When Robin
was murdered by Elizabeth it was Little John who
buried him.

EPILOGUE

Villains come in all shapes and sizes, from school bullies who will knock out your teeth for a bag of sweets, to 'great leaders' whose orders lead to misery for millions. Now you have some idea about how some villains became villains. But would you want to copy them? If YOU fancy a bit of murder and mayhem just remember, it's not all fun and games.

SOME villains can end up happy ever after. Captain Henry Morgan (1635–1688) was a Welsh sea captain who became a pirate. After years of robbery he settled down. He was made 'Sir' Henry by King Charles II and sent to govern Jamaica. Happy ending… Of course he died horribly from drinking too much rum, but there are lots of worse ways to go.

Most villains bring misery, suffering and death to the world … then end up miserable, suffering and dead.

Villains have been …

Boiled alive

Hanged

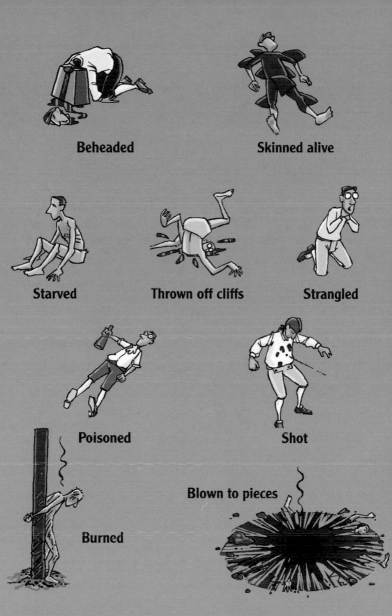

Beheaded

Skinned alive

Starved

Thrown off cliffs

Strangled

Poisoned

Shot

Blown to pieces

Burned

Villainy seems fun when you're winning ... but you end up making so many enemies they get you in the end.

Is it worth it?

INDEX